THE ALL NEW STYLE OF MAGAZINE-BOOKS

SDM

www.SDMLIVE.com

MP

MOCY PUBLISHING
WWW.MOCYPUBLISHING.COM

THE *Rashelle Rey* SHOW

PREMIERING
SEPTEMBER 13TH

Tyria Thomas
SPECIAL GUEST

COMING SOON IN SEPTEMBER MONDAY - FRIDAY AT 11AM EST

SDM on ROKU TV

SDM

EDITOR-IN-CHIEF
D. "Casino" Bailey
casino@sdmlive.com

EDITORIAL DIRECTOR
Sheree Cranford
sheree@sdmlive.com

GRAPHIC/WEB DESIGNER
D. "Casino" Bailey
casino@sdmlive.com

A&R MANAGER
Aye Money
ayemoney@sdmlive.com

ACCOUNT EXECUTIVE
Frank Harvest Jr.
frank@sdmlive.com

PHOTOGRAPHERS
Treagen Colston
D. "Casino" Bailey

CONTRIBUTORS
April Smiley
Courtney Benjamin

COPY ORDERS & ADVERTISING OFFICE
Send Money Order or Check to:
Mocy Publishing
P.O. Box 35195
Detroit, Michigan 48235
(586) 646-8505
advertise@sdmlive.com

Copy Order Item #:
SDM Magazine Issue #10 2016
S&H Plus Retail Price - $9.99 per copy

WWW.SDMLIVE.COM

Printed by CreateSpace, An Amazon.com Company

MP
MOCY PUBLISHING

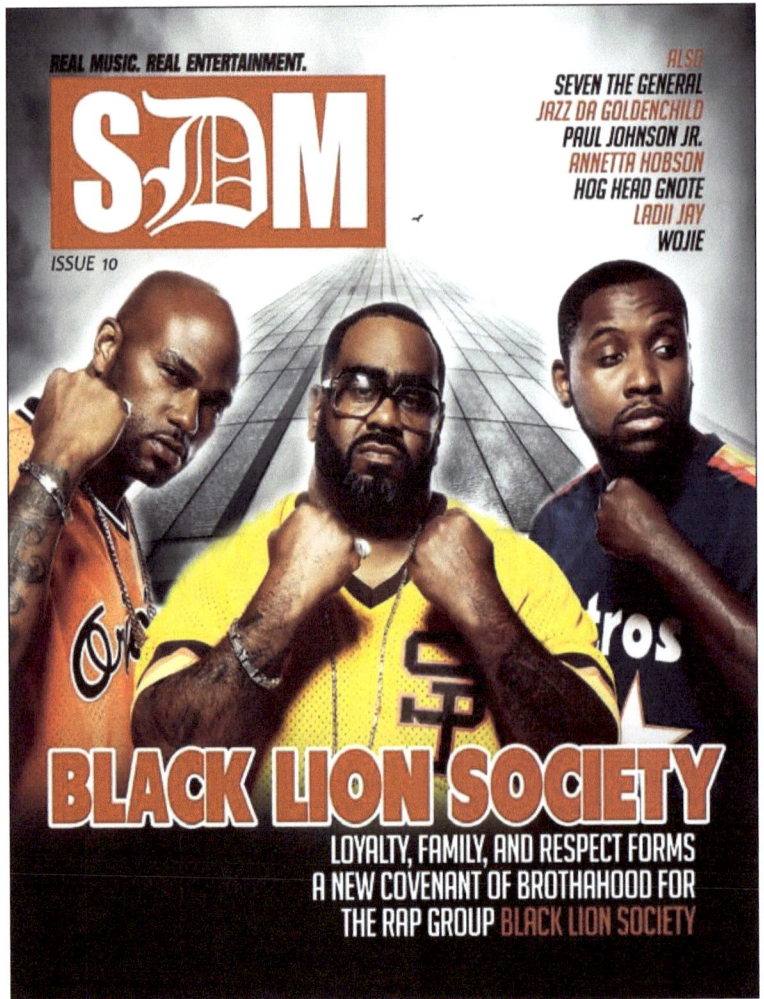

REAL MUSIC. REAL ENTERTAINMENT.

SDM
ISSUE 10

ALSO
SEVEN THE GENERAL
JAZZ DA GOLDENCHILD
PAUL JOHNSON JR.
ANNETTA HOBSON
HOG HEAD GNOTE
LADII JAY
WOJIE

BLACK LION SOCIETY
LOYALTY, FAMILY, AND RESPECT FORMS
A NEW COVENANT OF BROTHAHOOD FOR
THE RAP GROUP BLACK LION SOCIETY

ISSUE 10 - 2016

CONTENTS

1

Insignia™ - 39" Class (38.5" Diag.) - LED - 1080p - Smart - HDTV Roku TV - Black
$249.99
www.bestbuy.com

2

Microsoft - Xbox One S 2TB Console
$399.99
www.bestbuy.com

3

LG - Ultra Slim 8x Max. DVD Write Speed External USB DVD±RW/CD-RW Drive - Black
$29.99
www.bestbuy.com

Louisiana is Under Water

THE STATE OF LOUISIANA IS UNDER A FLASH FLOODING WATCH AND IS ONCE AGAIN EXPERIENCING AN HISTORIC, FATAL WEATHER DISASTER

by Cheraee C.

Unfortunately, for Louisiana another disaster has struck and President Obama just recently declared a state of emergency in agreeance with the Louisiana government officials. The floods are a trembling and devastating reminder of all the loss and damage that the state faced back in 2005 from Hurricane Katrina.

Over 20,000 people have been rescued from emergency crews, eleven deaths have been reported, over 40,000 homes and businesses have been damaged, and rescue workers are still working hard to save people. The government has deployed many soldiers from the National Guard to assist with this disaster. People have to say goodbye once again to their houses, their belongings, to their businesses, and live in overcrowded shelters, but at least they still have life. Still more rain is predicted in the forecast from a storm heading from the Gulf Coast to the Ohio Valley. So far more than 30 inches of rain has fallen in Southern Louisiana over the past week, and the National Weather Service reports Watson with the highest amount of rain of 31.4 inches. Sea levels are at an all-time high and at risk of becoming even higher. Who knows when the floods and sea levels will decrease?

Louisiana is a defenseless state that is susceptible to flash flooding because of its constant rising sea levels and it's low-lying land.

Hopefully the rain will pass, because Louisiana has a lot of restoring, rebuilding, and regrouping to do.

The Scarface Saga Returns

AUTHOR STANLEY L. BATTLE RETURNS WITH SCARFACE 2 WITH A PLOT OF EMOTIONAL AND CRIMINAL INTENSITY.

by Cheraee C.

Antonio Montero's son was young and feeble in Scarface Part 1, but in this grimey continuation it breaks down his stepfather's (Shawn Bomosk) downfall, and his godfather's (Alvin Stone) uprising, as Antonio experiences loss, racism, and matures into a wealthy man of power.

After graduating high school with a Porsche, Antonio decides that he wants to be apart of the infamous drug cartel hailing from Columbia led by Sorcerer. If only Antonio knew the true identity and cold realities of the man he was trapping for, he probably would've picked another career and went to college. Only time, Antonio's darkest times will reveal to him the naked truth. Will Antonio survive a mind of revenge, countless enemies, and a great state of depression?

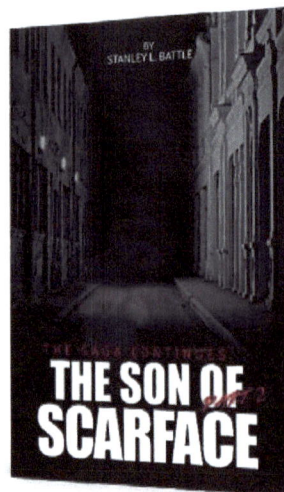

Scarface Part 2
By Stanley L. Battle

Available from Amazon.com and other online stores

TOP 10 COUNTDOWN
MUSIC VIDEOS
FRIDAYS & SATURDAYS
9PM EST

Hosted by
BINO THE PERSONALITY

SDM on **Roku TV**

Black Lion Musical Supremacy

THE THREE TALENTED RAPPERS JAKE DIAMONDZ, BIG SCAM, AND PHENOM ARE FINALLY FAMOUS AS THEY TAKE THEIR MOVEMENT ACROSS THE COUNTRY.

by Cheraee C.

Q. Who are all the members of Black Lion Society and what made y'all decide to become an unity?

A. Big Scam Jake Diamondz, Phenom. I've known Scam for years now and have always been a admirer of his movement. I met Jake when I became apart of our previous label and we all just clicked. We've been a group since 2012.

Q. How long have y'all been a group and what made y'all choose the name Black Lion Society?

A. We started out as Black Guvernment Gang and 2 years later changed our name after leaving our former label because of a conflict of interest for reasons not really worth mentioning. But I will say it was one of the best moves we made. Business wise, career wise, and personally.

Q. This year Black Lion Society was honored at the Underground Hip Hop Awards. What award did y'all receive and how did this honor make y'all feel?

A. We received the award for Best Group. It was absolutely an honor! And most definitely a confidence booster! To receive this award to us meant all our hard work along with our talent were most definitely weren't being overlooked! Especially with all the term oil we have been through and the recent name change, it was quite empowering to know the people were still rocking with us!

Q. Was this the first honor Black Lion Society received and what other awards and honors in Detroit are y'all aiming for?

A. This was our first time receiving an award, but in 2015 we were nominated in 5 categories at the Underground HipHop Awards. We're aiming for every category! We're pretty well rounded Artist...from lyricists to great stage presence. I'm sure in the near future we'll be bringing home more awards to decorate our studio.

Q. Music groups always clash and end up breaking up and sometimes never reconciling. How does your group plan to beat the odds of music group break-ups and conflicts?

A. (Jake Diamondz) We are around each other almost everyday and if not every other day. This music business will break the strongest relationships down true indeed, but the three of us have survived the ups and downs of going through the group change thing. We stat prayed up and we all rely on each other as a crutch when it comes to pushing one another. We've been around each other forever so we tend to be in tune with the individuals personal character as well as the artist...

(Big Scam) We are FAMILY FIRST so any conflict is handled as such, learn how to agree to disagree has been the best learning experience... Don't get me wrong cause niggaz get in their feelings and be on some bullshit but we understand that we are all that we got... We are overlooked alot but honestly there is no other underground group that has accomplished half as much as we have thus far, no disrespect to anyone but it is what it is...

(Phenom) Like all groups and families... we have our differences, but we also understand the value of family first! We have good business since as well as a open line of communication and we respect each other. These are my brothers! And blood couldn't make them any closer than we are now! At the end of the day we lean on each other for support... not just in music, but just as much in our personal situations. We have genuine love for one another and understand 100% that any problem can be worked through as long as we are honest and our always willing to communicate no matter what it is.

6. So Big Scam, Phenom, and Jake tell us about your daily struggles and hustles as individuals.

(Jake Diamondz) I'm a full time DHL employee, I work afternoons so most of the time when I would love to be in the studio working I'm at work working (lol) to help provide for my family and the music career. I also help take care of my mother and my grand mother so my life is non stop 24/7.

(Big Scam) My struggle starts at 6am every morning I'm up tending to my family and making sure that every one is okay... Then it's off to work dealing with these muthafuckaz and their lack of knowledge which makes my days often long and stressful... Then it's the pressure of the music and the things you have to do in the biz everyday> listen to beats, finish verses, talk to manager, speak with investors, locate graphics and photos, read thru show emails from promoters, read and understand paperwork, this is daily things we do... Mind you I didn't mention record!!! As a group we been hit with lots death and mishaps this year... We lost our sister Hazel at the beginning of the year followed shortly by Phenoms mom, Jake grandma had to undergo surgery and his mom was hospitalized and I almost lost my grandmother a lil while back so we have a lot going on all while making incredible music...

(Phenom) Before I'm Phenomm1 I'm Clinton. I'm a

father, a roll model and provider. I often struggle with balance of these things and try not to fall short in any of them! I lost my mother in April and that is the hardest thing I've had to deal with ever! My brothers Scam and Jake and the mother of my children have been the ppl who kept my head together and most of all our heavenly father who has blessed me countless times! I'm sure I speak for all of us when I say the pressure of being such unique artists in Detroit and being so different amongst fellow artist plays apart as well. Not many in the city do the level of music we do and a lot of the time our level of professionalism goes over artists heads as well as the typical Detroit consumer. On and off stage, behind or in front of the mic. We don't make music for the city...we make it for the world and that alone is were we differ from a lot of our peers. Its a problem for some and its a threat to many. But either way we will always do us to the fullest!

Q. How do y'all feel about all the presence of rap beefs in Detroit? Whether they are petty/uneccessary or publicity stunts?

(Jake Diamondz) Me personally I think some are for publicity and others are very unnecessary but, who am I to judge.

(Phenom) I feel that most of the rap beefs in the city are very senseless and insignificant! At the end of the day most of us are this for the love of music and to get rich! At least comfortable. The beefs here are shallow. Some even driven off ego's of ppl that smell themselves to much! But mostly its jealousy! The sad part is most of the ppl that are needing aren't as hot as they portray themselves to be. It makes us all look bad at the end of the day because it shows no unity amongst us. It's all petty to me...especially when there's no money being made!

(Big Scam) I think rap battles are health for the culture sewing that this is a gladiator sport... Emceeing was always about whose the best on the mic with more style and flyer than most... On the other hand Rap and Beef shouldn't be mentioned in the same sentence, shit they don't go together... You rap cause you Love/Like music, you Beef cause you dislike/hate something or someone... It gets messy when you got niggaz in they feelings getting personal and wanna fight cause a nigga got the best of you on the mic... Leave the personal shit outta of it (Mothers,Kids,Birth Disorders) if you ugly and can't dress fresh that's on you... The city doesn't need any help with senseless murder or gunfire blamed on music, how shallow is that... We all as artist should be concerned with getting the sound of the city together we've been sending out pissed poor music for years let the industry tell it... Beefing stops your money in music by way of corporate investments and sponsors they won't take a risk on getting a black eye on their name

Q. So where exactly are y'all from and what cities other then Detroit support y'all the most?

(Jake) I'm from Detroit born and raised. I grew up in the McDonald Square Projects, some of us call it Black Bottom. We've received the most love I think in the Carolinas they really rock with us out there but every city we touch we leave our mark there.

(Scam)I'm from Joy Rd the end that covers Livernois to Schaefer... We get alot of love from Wichita, Kansas they really rock with us heavy... We really like those small markets because the show are so intimate, it's like being on stage in front of your whole family... One giant musical family reunion...

Phenom is from Joy Rd as well, born and rasied.. Vegas has been showing us a lot of love as well as Toronto and Milwaukee.

Q. If y'all can improve one thing about today's music industry, what would it be?

(Jake) I would get rid of all these 360 deals, these dudes are going bankrupted years after they get

signed because of these deals and lack of knowledge for the music business.

(Scam) I want to change the way the music industry pays the artist while downplaying the artist worth... Plus in a working field such as music with all the traveling and risk taking their needs to be health care involved.

Phenom: The garbage ass artists that are being excepted, I feel it's cheapening our craft and making hip hop look like a joke.

SDM is the new movement taking over Detroit. Do y'all think Detroit needs a movement and what was the last movement you recall in Detroit?

(Jake)Detroit most definitely needs a movement because it's a lot of talent here that doesn't get the proper exposure necessary to take it to the next level. Honestly I can't think of the last strong movement that we had here besides when we were with Black Guvernment.

(Scam) Yes the city deserves a movement something like a couple of years ago Chicago had their time in the spot like... Our momentum is up and we have several acts making noise, but the key part is will we support one another to certify that we are a movement to be taken serious...

Phenom: Yes, Detroit most definitely needs a movement! Something positive and heavy at the same time. The last movement of any significance in Detroit in my own opnion was "No Fly Zone." Although it had mixed feelings from the consumers, it was very powrful and I feel Detroit gained a lot of support and respect because of it. Shoutout to the big homie Trick Trick and the whole GSM Squad!

Writing Scripts and Dominating Stages

PAUL JOHNSON JR. IS AN AMBITIOUS ACTOR, PLAYWRIGHT, AND DIRECTOR WHO IS EMBLESHING IN THE RISE OF DETROIT'S BLACK HOLLYWOOD SECTOR.

by **Cheraee C.**

Q. As an actor, playwright, and director do you feel like its a rise or fall of theater, film, or plays in our city?

A. Definitely a rise. Detroit is and always will be one of the best kept secrets when it comes to actors in theater and their abilities to bring character to the stage. As far as for film, we dropped the ball a few years back, but we have not failed as an industry city. As a matter of fact they are still shooting big movies here.

Q. What was the last play you directed and give a brief summary of what it was about?

A. My last stage production was entitled, "Ain't Been Gettin' None Lately." This was about three couples younger, middle-aged, and seniors based on 1 Corinthians 5:7. Basically, the play goes into each individual and how they choose to deal with sexual incompatibility.

Q. How did you get into acting and when did you have your first break?

A. I starting acting at Evangel Ministries under a lady named Judy. She was head of theater ministry. I played Charlie, a boy bound to a wheelchair who sang. This was in the late nineties. My big break came in 09' when I was asked to become part of the cast of "Kwame A River 11, The Wrath of Conyers," a satire type theatrical play written by one of the writers of SNL and Second City. It poked fun at Kwame Kilpatrick and Monica Conyers as they faced scrutiny and jailtime. This was when I knew I could write a play just as good or if not better. Twenty stage plays and here I am.

Q. Besides acting, what other talents do you have and what are your current interests?

A. I'm a singer, songwriter, music producer, media graphics, barber, and I'm also getting more into philanthropy. I'm in the process of starting my youth nonprofit organization.

Q. If I'm coming to see a Paul Johnson Jr play what can I expect that sets your shows apart from other playwrights?

A. A different storyline, surprise plot, and twists. My actors never turn their back, they project their voice, and have an overall standard and regard for the stage. My cast usually gels like family and that's what you see. Also, you see diversity. Not the same "Mama I spilled the Grits" type of stage plays.

Seven Remains The Street's General

SEVEN SPEAKS ON HIS EXPERTISE IN THE MUSIC INDUSTRY AND MUSIC BUSINESS AS HE MAKES HIS EXPERIENCES AND GIFTS WORK FOR HIM SINCE 07'.

by Cheraee C.

Q. Why do you call yourself Seven the General and how long have you been in the music industry?

A. I was named Young 7 Mile by older gangsters from my neighborhood. In prison I'm known as the general based on my actual position and ways I've layed plays down leads others to call me that.. i have references if needed. I've been in the industry professionally since 2007.

Q. What do you think is your biggest fanbase and what's the significance of your biggest fanbase?

A. My biggest fanbase are prisons. I spent almost 10 years there for a capital offense that I didn't commit at 17 years old. Other big fanbases I have are colleges, the streets, and overseas. Their significant because their support remains consistent.

Q. How do you feel that the Detroit music scene has changed since 2007?

A. Its majority streaming and YouTube now which is cool. It cost a lot more to be in this business in 07. Today you no longer need a brick and mortar establishment to move product. Just set-up a site and let it bang.

Q. Your songs are very constructive and contain the metaphors, analogies, and similies etc. Do you think other artists treat rapping with similar respect for the craf or just rap for recognition, a hobby, money, etc?

A. Well I can't speak for someone else. Sometimes it seems that way, but I believe it's just the youth in an artist and what he/she wants out of life. I came up battle rapping so everyday I had to be ready for war which I was. Undefeated 94-03 so by now it's my natural flow. I also study not just my craft, but the business. Not the industry, but the business because most don't know or understand the business of music where as I have a Bachelors Degree in Music Business!

Q. You've been in the industry a long time. I know you've seen a lot of rappers come and go. How do you feel about rap beefs and just staying out the way and doing your music?

A. Outisde of battle rap, I never got into the beef on wax with dudes. I'm too old and I take threats seriously so I made it a point to always show respect to everyone first and foremost. I speak to people as if they are just as important as I believe myself to be.

Q. What new music have you been working on and what can we look forward too from Seven for the remainder of this year. Do you have any ventures going on other then music such as movies etc?

A. In October I will be inducted into the Detroit Institute of Arts along wih Nick Speed, Guilty Simpson, Phat Kat, Hex Murder, and Denaun Porter as official legends of

Detroit Music in Hip Hop. The exhibit is: Detroit After Dark starts 10/21/16 at the DIA and runs through April 2017. The photographer Jenny Risher had four prints including ours purchased by the DIA for their permanent archive. I currently have finished an ablum entitled "Svengali" fear my latest song and video "4 the Low." It is being mastered as Nick Speed and I work on the follow up to our last project entitled ART2. I recently worked on Bizarre (D12) upcomng project Tweak Sity 2 as well as Kuniva D12 upcoming project A History of Violence 2. I just did some work on Boldy James and DJ Butters upcoming The Art of Rock Climbing all of which are coming soon. I have an exclusive release coming with and through the blog site The Smoking Section and many more collaborations and projects that I'm working off. As far as for films I just did the voiceover for the animated version of The Supreme Team based on Supreme McGriff out of New York. I do the voice of Supreme and Phat Kat with my brother B-Down The Boss directed by Al Profit and Seth. I also released the documentary for my album art as well as another documentary based on the life and writings of Donald Goines.

Two is Better Then One

WARNER BROTHERS MUSIC GROUP AND VEVO HAVE JOINED FORCES.

by Semaja Turner

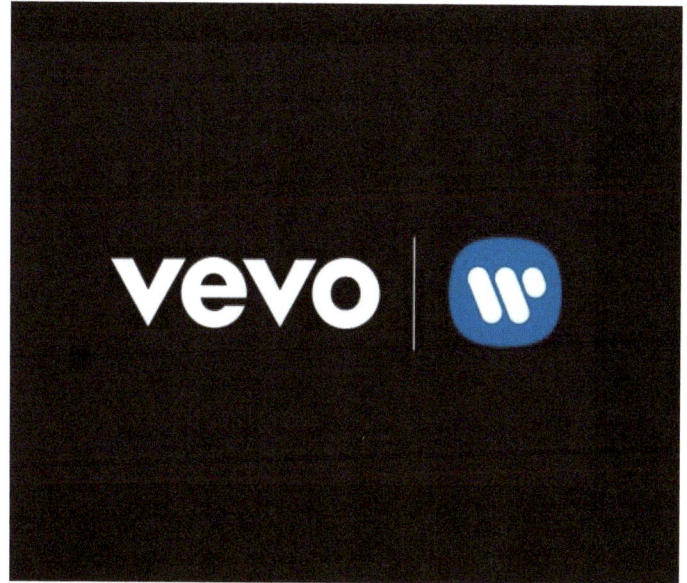

As great as pure independence is, there's nothing better then a good partnership. The latest partnership in the music industry is between Warner Brothers Music Group and Vevo. This wasn't an easy partnership and licensing deal to establish either. Apparently Warner Brothers has been undecisive with sealing the deal with Vevo for over a year now. Also, Warner Brothers is the last major label in the industry to team up with Vevo.

Finally, Warner Brothers decided to establish a video platform which is owned by a handfull of keyplayers in the music industry. The list includes, Universal Music Group, Sony Music Entertainment, Abu Dhabi Music, and Google. Unlike deals that have been made with other partners, this is not an equity deal, and the agreement excludes Youtube which gives Warner's artists complete ownership of their own Youtube channels.

The goal of the partnership is to provide music content from top Warner Brother's artists, and distribute that music across all of Vevo's internal and visual platforms. All Warner Brothers and Vevo want to do is continue to put their artists first and keep music alive.

Rip the Runaway with Ladii Jay

THE INSPIRATIONAL FASHION MOGUL LADII JAY TAKES HER FASHION STATEMENT TO EVENTS, RADIO STREAMS, AND THE RUNAWAYS OF DETROIT.

by Cheraee C.

Q. Who is Ladii Jay as an entreprenuer and what specific fields do you specialize in?

A. Ladii jay is a model, runway coordinator, event planner and host. I am founder and C.E.O. of my own fashion
company "The Fashion Statement." We specialize in producing fashion events as well as runway training classes, building networking skills, and photography.

Q. How do you help other entreprenuers around Detroit and what inspired your leadership and organizational spirit?

A. I help other entrepreneurs by creating a medium through which they connect with people they wouldn't otherwise be exposed to. What really sparked my leadership skills at a young age was being a JROTC cadet for 4 years. I was taught how to stay focused on set goals and not break under pressure. The program also helped me highten my organization skills due to having to be in charge of large groups of people and ensuring that everyone is on the same page at the same time. I also just have a love for planning and bringing people together for a common purpose.

Q. As an event planner describe the biggest event you planned?

A. The biggest event that I have ever planned was my very first company production on August 7th, 2016. It was a 16 designer showcase that featured High fashion, urban fashion, menswear, and kidswear. I was blessed to have an awesome production team as well as a host of mua's, hairstylists, photographers, bloggers, vendors, and volunteers. I sold out of seats and had standing room only! I must say, I was very satisfied with the turn out, especially because it was my first official production!

Q. Describe the radio show you host and yourself as a radio personality?

A. The radio show I host is called "Destined For Greatness." I co-host with Mo'Nae Rawls The Media Diva through
Motor City Woman Radio. We talk about community issues, entertainment, politics, and current events

happening in the Detroit area. We like to do guest interviews on the show with locals that are doing great things that deserve to be promoted.

Q. As a woman into fashion and entertainment, where do you see yourself in the fashion and entertainment world in the next 2 years?

A. In the next two years I plan to have expanded my company outside of Michigan, making a networking gateway for many models and designers in different states. I would hope that in the next two years, people will be able to reflect on my work and use it as their inspiration to chase after and pursue their dreams just like me!

Annetta "the literary innovator" Hobson

CO-OWNER OF AVOC PUBLISHING AND AUTHOR HELPS CREATE THE BIGGEST BOOK FESTIVAL IN MICHIGAN AND IS CREATING NEW OPPORTUNITIES FOR AUTHORS

by Cheraee C.

Q. How long have you been writing and how long have you been a published author?
A. I began writing in May of 2012. I sent my first manuscript out that August. I got two offers and was signed October 2012.

Q. What type of publishing company is Donnaink Publications and why did you stop publishing with them?
A. DonnaInk Pub was a publishing company ran by a woman that wanted to try and publish the traditional way. Things started out great and ended up going south. Promises were not kept and some internal things caused her to file bankruptcy and change her LLC.

Q. When did you team up with AVOC Publishing and what is the overall mission for authors there?
A. My sister and i decided that we should start our own company who could serve you and make sure that you're treated right better than yourself. Our mission is to be upfront and honest with authors. We want their publishing fantasies to be fulfilled without killing their dreams.

Q. Who started the Motor City Experience and how has the Motor City Book experience impacted the writing world?
A. I wanted to do a fair in Detroit a few years ago in 2014, but couldn't find a decent venue. But while in New York we, AVOC Publishing, and Kenerly Presens came up with the idea of the Motor City Book Experience and decided to put it in motion in 2015. I don't know how it will impact the writing world yet. But I hope it brings Detroit or Michigan authors together and makes an impact on the literary world.

Q. You've got a huge book event, a publishing company, and a radio show. Tell us about your radio show and what other platforms you are creating for authors.?
A. I want authors to be able to appear on our show and be in a relaxed, fun atmosphere. We want our show to be enjoyable and something that people other than just authors and readers can tune into.

TOP 10 CHARTS

TOP 10 DIGITAL SINGLES AND ALBUMS
SEPTEMBER 1, 2016

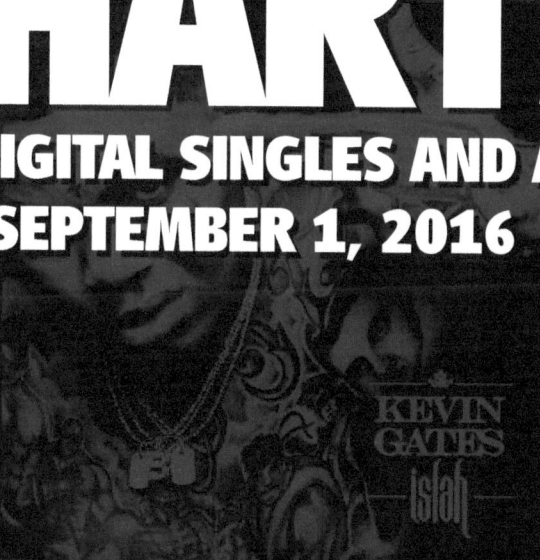

TOP 10 CHARTS

DJ KHALED WITH OTHER RAP LEGENDS ON THE VIDEO SET "I GOT THE KEY".

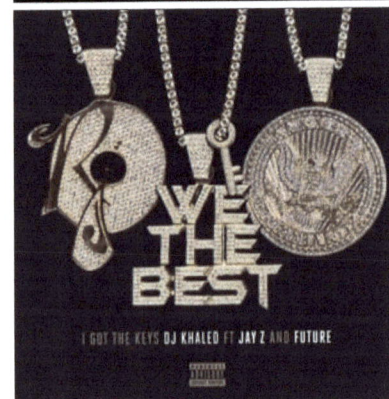

DJ Khaled
I Got The Keys

Coming in at #1 this month, DJ Khaled is letting the world know about all of his keys.

TOP 10 SINGLES
CHART OF THE MONTH

No.	Artist - Song Title
1	DJ KHALED - I GOT THE KEYS
2	FUTURE - WICKED
3	MADEINTYO - UBER EVYERWHERE
4	FAT JOE FT. REMY MA - ALL THE WAY UP
5	DRAKE - CONTROLLA
6	T.I. FT. MARSHA AMBROSIUS - DOPE
7	DJ KHALED FT. DRAKE - FOR FREE
8	50 CENT FT. CHRIS BROWN - I'M THE MAN (REMIX)
9	MOBDIVA - IS YOU ROLLIN
10	WALE - MY PYT

TOP 10 ALBUMS
CHART OF THE MONTH

No.	Artist - Album Title
1	DJ KHALED - MAJOR KEY
2	FANTASIA - THE DEFINITION OF.....
3	GUCCI MANE - EVERYBODY LOOKING
4	KEITH SWEAT - DRESS TO IMPRESS
5	RO JAMES - ELDORADO
6	KANYE WEST - THE LIFE OF PABLO
7	MAXWELL- BLACKSUMMERS'NIGHT
8	OT GENASIS - RHYTHM & BRICKS
9	SCHOOLBOY Q - BLANK FACE LP
10	KING DILLON - THE CORONATION

TOP 3 ALBUMS THIS MONTH

Major Key

ARTIST: DJ Khaled
REVIEWER: Cheraee C.
RATING: 5

The hottest DJ in the nation is returns with major keys on his latest album. Tracks include I Got The Keys featuring Jay-Z and Future, For Free featuring Drake, Nas Album Done featuring Nas, Work For It featuring Big Sean, Gucci Mane, and 2 Chainz, Ima Be Alright featuring Bryson Tiller and Future, Do You Mind featuring Nicki Minaj, Chris Brown, August Alsina, Jeremih, Future, and Rick Ross, and many more hot tracks. I give the album five stars.

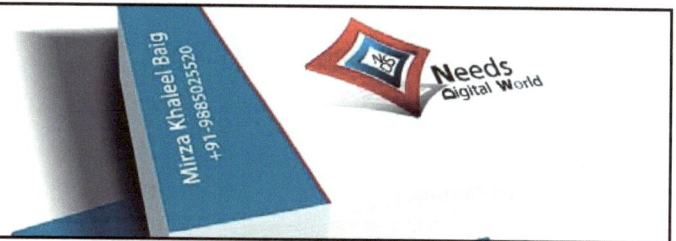

RATE METER: 1 - WACK   2 - NEEDS WORK   3 - STRAIGHT   4 - BANGER   5 - CLASSIC

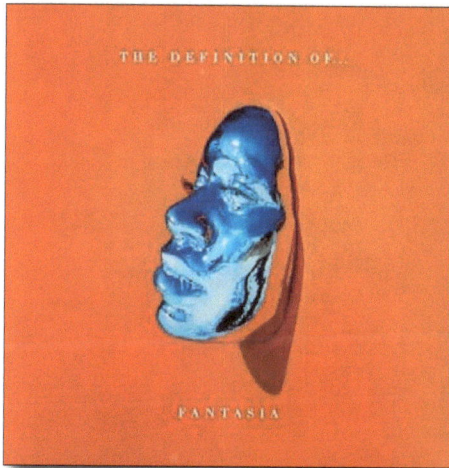

The Definition of...

ARTIST: Fantasia
REVIEWER: Cheraee C.
RATING: 3

R&B sensation and soul-survivor Fantasia is ready to show fans the true definition of her with her brand new album. Hit singles from the album include Sleeping With The One I Love, Wait For You, I Made It featuring Tye Tribbett, Stay Up featuring Stacy Barthe, and Roller Coasters featuring Aloe Blacc. I give the album four stars.

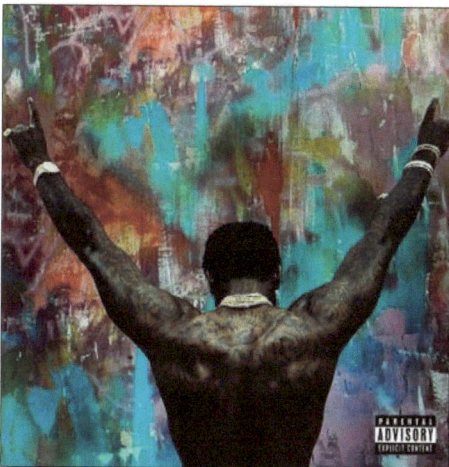

Everybody Looking

ARTIST: Gucci Mane
REVIEWER: Cheraee C.
RATING: 3

When Gucci was in prison, his release was most wanted, now that he's out, his latest album was most wanted as well. Hot tracks include Pussy Print featuring Kanye West, Out Do Ya, Robbed, Richest Niggas in the Room, and many other tracks. I give this album three stars.

A Real OG to The Rap Game

HOG HEAD GNOTE EXPLAINS HOW HE WAS PRONOUNED DEAD IN HIGH SCHOOL JUST TO COME BACK TO LIFE WITH A WHOLE NEW DIRECTION.

by Cheraee C.

Q. Why do you call yourself Hog Head Gnote and how would you best describe your music?

A. Well Hog Head Entertainment is the record company and I was given the name Gnote from one of the homies. My music is a mix of day to day things in life that we all go through, telling different parts of stories in my life experiences.

Q. What is one of the craziest experiences you've been through in life that you have or will rap about?

A. When I was an active gang banger I got shot in my stomach inside Northern High School and I was pronounced dead on the scene. I was 15 years old and my friend bought it in for a hit on me and he was false flagging and took up the offer.

Q. How did you get into rap and rapping? Was it your surroundings or something you was born to do?

A. I started rapping at 7 years old from my big brother best friend who at the time was Obie Trice. We use to be on his front porch rapping for hours and hours nonstop and he always said he was goin be a rapper and that made me want to be one and then I was introduced to the drug game by my father, a Detroit Northend Legend as he was one of the first to introduce marijuana over there in that community. Also, he started a lot of big names off in the game as drug dealers and he taught me the game at an early age. Before I knew it me and my bros were 12 years old selling drugs in and out of town gang banging, robbing,, and carjacking just for fun.

Q. How do you feel about the new generations of rap? Do you think rap is more of an outlet or a career to them?

A. I think the new rap is garbage music without any substance or value and a lot of the rappers aren't going to be relevant in the next 5-10 years. I think rap is neither an outlet nor a career; it's just something for them to do.

HEELS &
SKILLZ

Faren

is a beautiful model
from Orlando, FL.

instagram
@missfarenw

Photography by
@barearmy

HEELS & SKILLZ

Cristina Cold
is a full-time model from Detroit, MI.

instagram
@cristinacold2

Cheraee's Corner

WHY IS IT IMPORTANT FOR BLACK PEOPLE TO VOTE?

by **Cheraee C.**

Once upon a time, voting wasn't a right or privilege for people of color. Now who are we as citizens in a new era even more diverse as people of color not to exercise a right that came with historical loss, bloodshed, war, and injustice. The wars that we had to win, weren't won just for bragging rights. They were won because every opinion matters and counts especially as it relates to society and the future of the next generation. All it takes is one opinion, one leader, or one man or woman to change the whole world.

Why is it that people will wait, starve, and faint for the new pair of Jordans, the Mega Million jackpot, or the new IPhone, but people don't treat voting the same way when voting is free? All voting takes is free will and a few minutes to fill out a voting ballet. To narrow it down to two main categories you either democratic or repuublican. Yet our mothers and fathers and elders have to force us to the polls, when we should be running to the polls as soon as they open happy that we can vote.

If we can have a black President that served two terms in office, nothing is impossible. People of color spend hours giving their opinions on other's peoples lives, choices, and decisions, yet the decision that really counts we hesitate to give our opnion of. If we care about who our President is, how much gas prices are, health care, world allliances, and etc then get out and vote whether voting pertains to local council and local judges, or Presidents and Vice Presidents.

NEXT 2 BLOW

JAZZ DA GOLDENCHILD

Q. **Why do you call yourself Detroit's Bostress?**
A. You are what you say you are.. I say I'm a star.. The name bosstress came over time of rapping. I'm not the mistress of Detroit, I'm the bosstress.. The name goes with my music which is powerful like my voice when people hear my voice, they automatically feel the power in my name.

Q. Do you feel like you chose rapping as a craft or rapping chose you?
A. I have always loved music since I was a little girl I would make my own versions of all my favorite songs.. I started writing poetry then at the age of 15 I got locked up in juvenile detention... I got talked about and I couldn't fight so I started battle rapping. I would kill um on the freestyle... It has always been in me even on my worst day when music turned it's back on me I still stayed loyal. That's my bitch lol it chose me.

Q. When and why do you feel like music turned its back on you?
A. Just a figure of speaking. What I mean is my musical journeyy has been filled with blood, sweat, and tears. My love of music made me vulnerable at one point... I wanted it so bad I thought that glitter was gold... Blind to the sharks in this business.. Music led me to dealing with all the wrong people in all the wrong places. I end up losing what I thought were friends we're actually out to use me... When you love something so much it's hard to believe there's any wrong in it.. Just like a mother who believes her child can do no wrong.

Q. Desribe yourself as an artist and your current feelings about breaking into the music industry?

A. As an artist I come as real as it gets. Growing up in poverty and facing many hardships is reflected in my lyrics. As many rules as there may be to this industry, I feel as if I'm an exception because whether you are a fan, meaning you relate to what I say on the record and willing to bump it, I know I will be respected for my talent and grind. As far as hip hop goes, it's a passion being able to describe how I feel at the time to a dope ass banging beat. I think the people will understand who I am as a person and be able to relate for I am not the only one who has been through life. Whether I'm happy, sad, or just standing my ground. Starting from poetry, I knew I am able to help others understand the feeling of whatever, and with that I just know that'll be my breakthrough... with the support of the fans, and for that I thank you.

Q. You said you started writing from poetry so do you consider music to be a form of poetry or should poetry and music be categorized separately?
A. Music is music and lyrics are a form of poetry.

Q. Do you feel like race, gender, class etc affect your survival and fame in the music industry?
A. I think we've come to a point where race is no longer an issue. Gender in hip hop comes with its stereotypes. I've been in a few situations where I wasn't taken seriously because I am a female, and I think alot of us female artists sruggle with that before we are known. I think class has alot to do with your survival in the game because it takes money to make money, and that ultimately has my been my issue, which is funding my craft. I feel even if you have money to live comfrotably, you should always respect the struggle . I know a lot of talented artists who are left behind because they have to work their 9-5's instead of being at the showcases and being seen. Fortunately for myself, I've been building a support team to help the exposure and were pulling together to get heard. If it's mean to be, the fame will find me.

WOJIE

SNAP SHOTS

Email Your Snap Shots to
snapshots@sdmlive.com

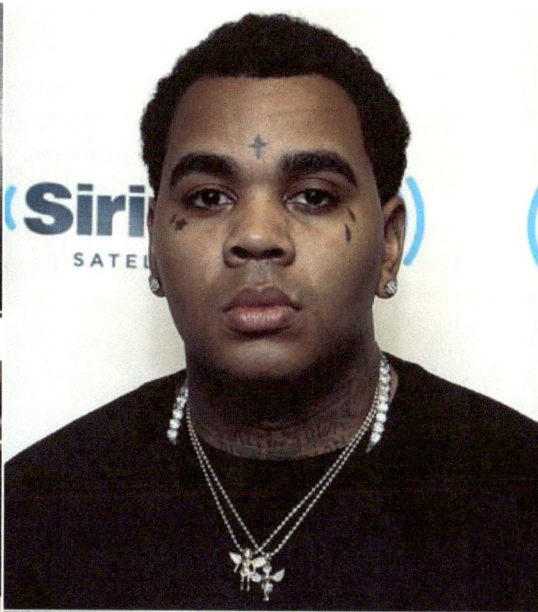

5DS PRODUCTIONS®
THE PRINT MEDIA CENTER.

PRINT

GET 10% OFF WITH CODE: SAVE10OFF

DIGITAL & PRESS RUN PRICE LIST

BUSINESS CARD 2x3.5 INCHES		TRIFOLD BROCHURE 8.5x11 INCHES		POSTCARDS 4x6 INCHES	
100	$10	250	$150	250	$50
500	$20	500	$180	500	$55
1000	$30	1000	$230	1000	$65
5000	$100	5000	$350	5000	$130
10000	$170	10000	$680	10000	$250

FLYERS - BROCHURES - BANNERS - BUSINESS CARDS - CD INSERTS CALENDARS - EVENT TICKETS - POSTCARDS - POSTERS YARD SIGNS - AND MUCH MORE

DIGITAL & PRESS RUN PRINTING

FAST TURN AROUND PRINTING

GET FREE SHIPPING ON ALL ORDERS

YOU SAVE MONEY WHEN YOU PRINT AT
WWW.THEPRINTMEDIACENTER.COM
24/7 ONLINE ORDERING. CALL US NOW 1.888.718.2999

COUPON CODE IS FOR A LIMITED TIME OFFER - FREE UPS SHIPPING ANYWHERE IN THE US

Urban Fiction, Spiritual, Motivation and more.
Order a book from Mocy Publishing today and receive FREE shipping.

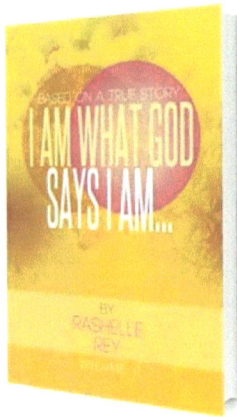

I Am What God Says I Am...
By Rashelle Rey

Item #: IAWGS29
Price: $9.99

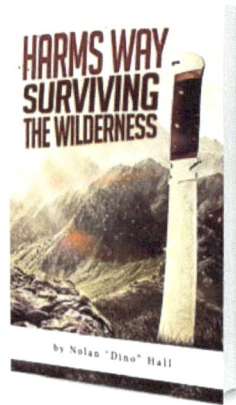

Harm's Way
By Nolan "Dino" Hall

Item #: HWS821
Price: $15.99

The Shadiest Mission Ever
By Cheraee C.

Item #: TSME28
Price: $12.99

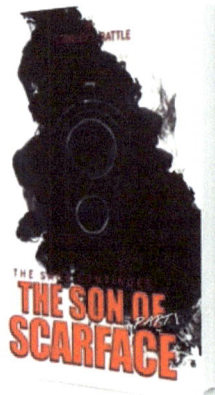

The Son Of Scarface – Part 1
By Stanley L. Battle

Item #: TSOS01
Price: $12.99

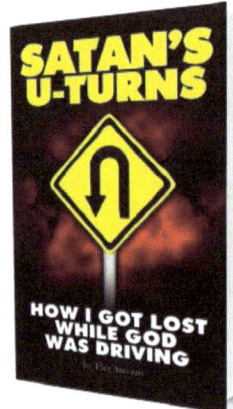

Satan's U-Turns
By Flex Stevens

Item #: SUT382
Price: $9.99

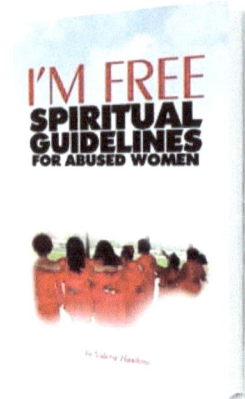

I'm Free
By Valerie Hawkins

Item #: IFTSG82
Price: $14.99

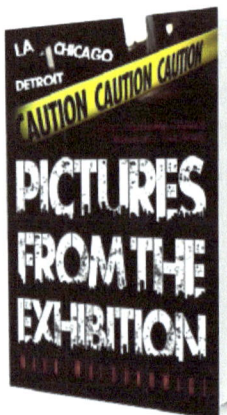

Pictures From The Exhibition
By Mark Wolodkowicz

Item #: PFAE292
Price: $15.99

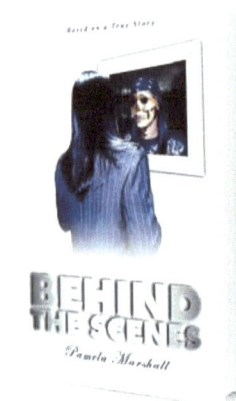

Behind The Scenes
By Pamela Marshall

Item #: BTS721
Price: $15.99

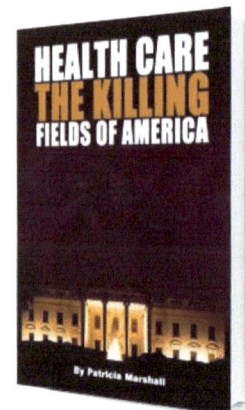

Health Care
By Patricia Marshall

Item #: HCTABF2
Price: $17.99

www.mocypublishing.com
order online and receive FREE shipping. Limit time offer.

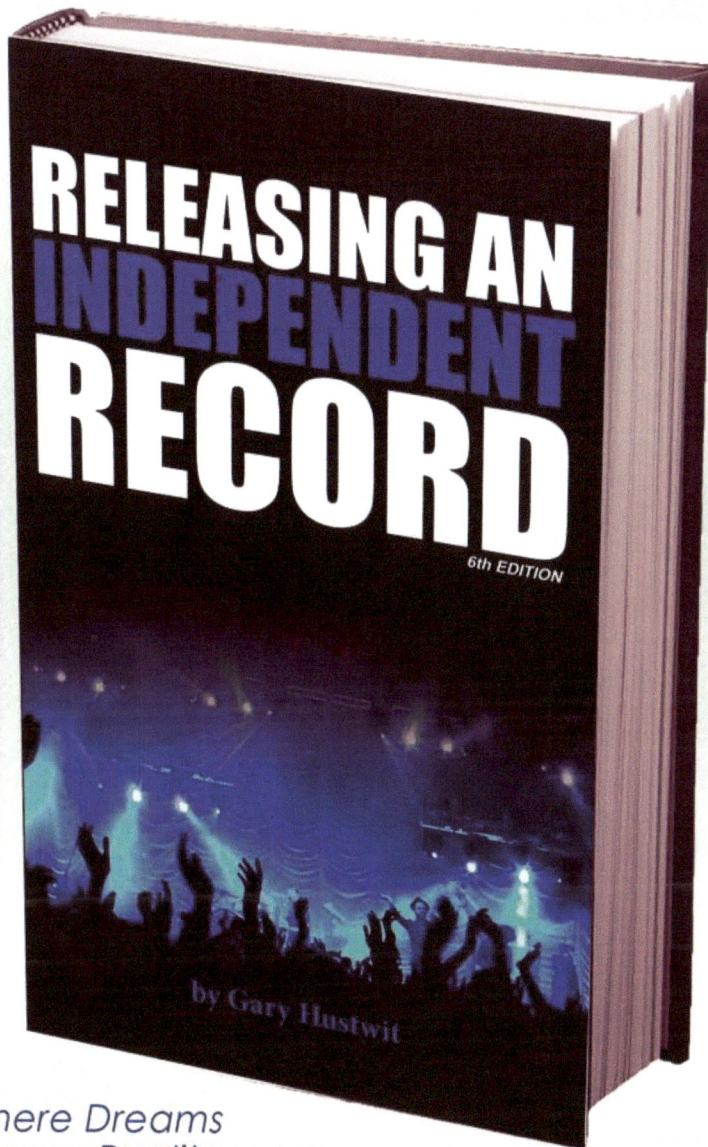

LOOKING FOR A NEW LOOK

LET US CREATE A NEW WEBSITE FOR YOUR COMPANY FOR LESS.

Basic

$3.99/month

1 Website
10 GB Storage
25,000 Monthly Vistors

PLUS

* FREE Monthly Hosting
* Get a FREE Domain
  with annual plan

Standard

$4.99/month

1 Website
15 GB Storage
100,000 Monthly Vistors

PLUS

* FREE Monthly Hosting
* Search engine
  optimization plugin
* Get a FREE Domain
  with annual plan

Premium

$12.99/month

1 Website
50 GB Storage
800,000 Monthly Vistors

PLUS

* FREE Monthly Hosting
* Search engine
  optimization plugin
* RapidSSL Certificate
* Get a FREE Domain
  with annual plan

We offer complete WordPress website design and development. From a simple website to an advanced business e-Commerce solution, we can create the ultimate solution to meet your marketing goals and objectives.

All of our custom website builds follow a structured development process which helps us execute your project on-time and on-budget. For prices go to www.5DShost.com/websites

5DSHOST
THE BEST FOR HOSTING

Call Our Support:
(888) 718-2999
WWW.5DSHOST.COM

REAL MUSIC. REAL ENTERTAINMENT.

S.DM

ISSUE 3

KOSTA
JUST HIT THE JACKPOT WITH A NEW SMASH HIT SINGLE "LOTTERY"

BIGG DAWG BLAST
LAUNCHES THE STREET HITTA DJ'S MOVEMENT

Neisha Neshae

BRINGING IN 2016 ON STAGE WITH THE KING OF R&B R-KELLY & DROPPING A NEW MIXTAPE

PLUS MORE

THE RED CARPET EDITION
SUPERSTARS CAME WITH FASHION AT THE SDM MAGAZINE RELEASE PARTY

US - $9.99 CANADA - $14.99

01 >

9 770317 847001

JANUARY 2016 No.3
WWW.SDMLIVE.COM

THE ALL NEW STYLE OF MAGAZINE-BOOKS

SDM

www.ingramcontent.com/pod-product-compliance
Lightning Source LLC
Chambersburg PA
CBHW040019050426
42452CB00002B/41